eggplants & teardrops:

a haiku collection

aaron barry

Makena:

for your endless charity

and love of humour

& a special thanks to Vicki, Nick, Antoinette, Kayla, Sage, John, and Liam.

First published 2022

ISBN 978-1-7386339-0-6

Independently published
Typeset and cover design by Liam Relph
Author photo by Connor Murphy
Illustrated by Eunbyul Kwak

Contents

Readers who know little about haiku, as well as those who are well informed about it, may ask if these poems are, indeed, haiku. But they will ask this question for very different reasons.

Those who think a haiku is a seventeen-syllable poem, structured in a three-line stanza, about almost any topic will not find these elements here. Additionally, those who know the developmental history of haiku in Japanese literature, and now in world literature, will be aware that the seventeen sound units of Japanese haiku are generally not replicated in other languages and are not definitive, even in Japan. These more informed readers will know that haiku in English may be written in one, two, three, or four lines, or even in brief conceptual arrangements and may feature a wide variety of Western poetic devices. But they will also know there is a Japanese poetic form called *senryu*, with exactly the same structure as haiku, and will recognize that a large portion of the poems in this book are, in fact, senryu.

The distinction between haiku and senryu is not based on form, but on subject matter, genre origins, emotional tone, and what each type of poetry attempts to offer the reader. If haiku celebrates and elevates life and nature, senryu is a converse that pokes fun at life and the various shades of the human condition. Both stem from the *haikai* tradition in Japan, which was known for its playfulness, puns, and raunchiness—and, as in this collection, it was not unusual for poets of the time to illustrate works of either kind with calligraphy or ink pictures. But with the advent of figures like Matsuo Bashō in the 17th century, a cultural shift saw preference given to serious poems that fell under the haiku banner.

Yet even for readers who have read Japanese- and English-language haiku and senryu widely, this book offers something from the edges, something new and thrilling. That's the result of a youthful, no-holds-barred approach from a similarly youthful author. Aaron Barry's truth is one that the poets of Matsuo Bashō's day surely had no conception of—one of social media, manga, and urban slang. It's a world of being broke, looking for love in all the wrong places, and living in a state of constant revision. It's an existence of conflicting nihilism and reckless optimism, occasional self-deprecation, and ironic social commentary. In this sense, Barry's work is an expression of the next generation's most distressing, beautiful, and vulgar experiences, rendered through an ancient poetic tradition.

In the editing process, I found it necessary to research terms from almost every poem—terms that help define a generation to which I do not belong. Generations of artists, though, are not chronologically discrete. Aaron and I came together not because our truths were similar, but because art transcends such considerations, and because the community of artists is based upon something far greater than a shared age. Just as I sought to create something new when I was working with the poets who came before me, Aaron Barry has written a collection that seeks to bring about a new iteration of haiku and senryu that doesn't shy away from the topics that truly matter to him and his Millennial/Gen Z contemporaries. And I believe his work has the power to draw in readers and other poets who may not know just how radically English-language haiku has changed in recent years.

But, most crucially, I regard this as an important book for the form because Aaron's approach honours our common goal, a goal nearly every writer of haiku and senryu shares today: to breathe new life into this incredible literary legacy.

John Stevenson

Former President, Haiku Society of America

Managing Editor, *The Heron's Nest*

opening (your) clam

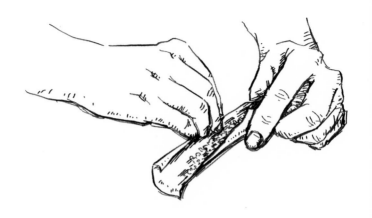

weed

   to put it

      bluntly

online dating—

here's to hoping

we click

quarter-life crisis…

she comes back

hyphenated

where the fuck

were you last night

day moon

fs in chat

for the autumn leaves

https://www.summerheatsquirrelsgonewild.com

zazen...

the fading ping

of a DM

oneness

the carpet = the drapes

tuition fees

another student

brought to their knees

a gingerbread house in this economy

post-postmodern exhibit[1]

---

[1]I pull my turtleneck[a]

[a]higher

climate change

make it two

popsicles

nearly out of sight smog

arguing

   in the zen forums

      over who's calmer

                  buddha you think you are buddy

anXIETY

first bloom

and the freedom

not to

express train the beverage cart taking forever

morning commute

who can play their podcast

loudest

The apparition of these faces in the crowd:

Petals on a wet *please stand behind the yellow line**

thrifting

how much for the

abandoned dream

his furry costume the elephant in the room

devil moon—

I leave the organics

unsorted

haiku me

like one of your

anime girls

what did you just say about my waifu

manga my like way wrong the her reading

reading her the wrong way like my manga

first anniversary

the length of our

snap streak

birdsong

the legato staccato crescendo ritardando of

my roommate's hookup

of all the days

for this to happen...

flow tide

breakup — maybe I am — bisexual

single star…

these teardrops

analog

in place of vulnerability persimmons

he / hymn / his

she / her / slurs

music festival

these outhouses

not a vibe

ocean sounds alba core

as the crow flies fentanyl

after sex

the mood turns

confessional

cherry blossoms

and the confession

I'm still waiting for

the talk...

dad actually uses the word

gazongas

mother's birthday—

time to think outside

the chocolate box

rebel phase

I tell grandma

to frick off

wild

flowers

this

time

away

from

family

his new goal

to get swole—

year of the pig

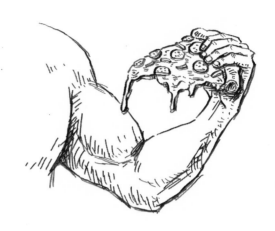

vegan muffins:

+2 health

−10 reputation

trail mix—

the teacher explains

multiculturalism

HaIkUs ArE eAsY

bUt SoMeTiMeS tHeY dOn'T mAkE sEnSe

ReFrIgErAtOr*

[fragment][punctuation]

[juxtaposed phrase within

established context]

[pick: *season*] [pick: *time of day*]

the [pick: *expletive*] [pick: *animal*]

won't [pick: *verb*]

no kigo, no problem

tired of the nature imagery

I pull up

a screen

dead sea don't give me any ideas

old diary

cringing at myself

cringing at myself

send pussywillow pics

of other lives

her cat

says nothing

water-into-wine o'clock

wicked hangover…

the roses

just roses today

writer's block…

_____

_____

finally ready

to use those three famous words…

saguaro blossoms

empty snail shell

another

foreclosure

steeped chamomile—

the nightingale's calls

go to voicemail

a dogwood petal

graces his fedora

euphoria

you son of a bitch I hope you chokecherries

depending on the time of day

aubergines

or eggplants

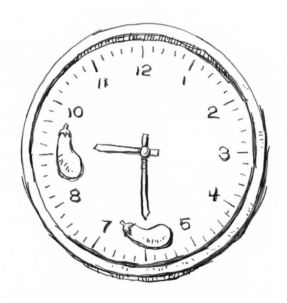

fresh mint

no way to make sense

of this loss

fresh sense no way to

make mint of this loss

no loss fresh this way to make sense of mint

night walk :: the void :: here

I type, erase, retype

Erase again, and then

I'm ghosted

(Katsushika Hokusai)*

.

Consider me

As one who loved poetry

And eating ass

(Masaoka Shiki)*

The light of a vape

Is transferred to another—

Spring twilight

(Yosa Buson)*

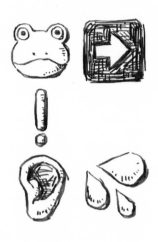

(Matsuo Bashō)*

two new matches

on Tinder!

harvest moon

mating season—

I send a

wyd

serotonin sun

   moon dopamine

                        iCloudy

sultry night

taking the shrink wrap off

my new body pillow

wet market

I've seen this

hentai before

yard sale:

peloton

never used

two kisses

obo

no clouds in sight…

I let the telemarketer

go on

#newalgorithm

#theadvertisersknowingmebetter

#thanme

shifting cumulus

we make plans

to make plans

yelp

these people

need help

youtube

not a single user

born in the right gen

boomerlogic2 (3 hours ago)

they sure don't write poems like they used to

👍 63   👎 1

glamping

between us and the mosquitoes

a class divide

midsummer sky

the goldfinch above

left and right

communist rally

every button sold

helps fight capitalism

conservative rally

the camo-print

petition

midsummer sky

the goldfinch beyond

left and right

the fireflies

almost as bright

as your gaslighting

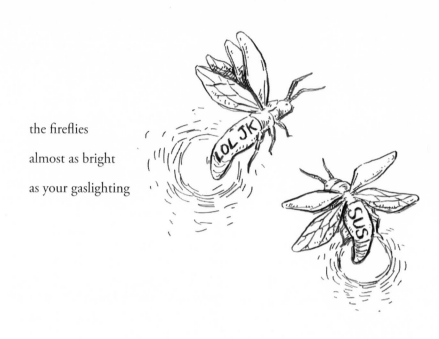

fish soup

from one vertebrate

to another

Indian summer—

I ask

for a to-go bag

catfishing for compliments

always the bridesmaid...

a release dove

fails to take flight

marriage proposal...

I'm feeling so many

emojis right now

rain

      dropping

all

      pretense

                                  aft er th e ra in

                                  ref ra cto ry per i od

dog attention hydrangea deficit

sunlight hyperactive breeze disorder

chicken bones already I feel like we

wait is this poem a death poem hypochondria

hipster café—

I think I've made

a grande mistake

a fine arts degree

I say

in my customer service voice

the name's frond—fern frond

community garden—

tell your kale

to stop bullying mine

beeth that

thy final wish

alfalfa

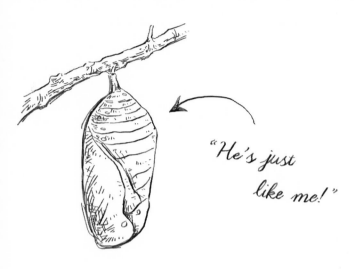

"He's just
like me!"

much like the pupa … introversion

coworker

posting #motivational content again…

tumbleweeds

logging in

seeing an old friend's message

about a ponzi scheme

logging out

among the whole lot

not a single astronaut—

high school reunion

recovery...

the condescension

of a smiley-faced balloon

you mockingbird little

mockingbird bastard

mockingbird I'll

therapy session

running out of synonyms

for *simp*

a k-pop stan & an e-girl walk into a karaoke bar...

dragonflies...

to defy

a name

van life

every day a different

~~adventure~~

parking lot

switching to hard mode foreign country

to show them I'm worldly I order the wasabi

you you you
hey you ^ polyamory

camellias

it's more of a

situationship

faulty condom…

ice forming

on the fire escape

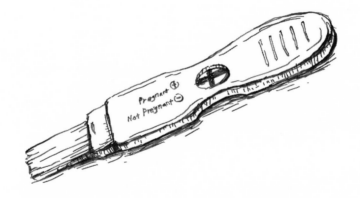

this is not   +

an exit   test

if it's easier for you no abortion

iiimnotddrunkuare... uber

resurrection day 3 of my bender

still

here

winter

daybreak

the rooster's

existentialism

hardcormorants

zaddy long legs*

thistle seed

the chickadee

living its best life

happy hour

if only

for the irony

one goose

getting roasted

in the group chat

sunflowers

the house spider

starting over

[forest walk I pretend not to see the cedar's stretch marks]

flicking through

the obituaries…

starry night

                                              light pollution or is orion

                                                        losing weight

titan orbiting saturn like a complete beta

with all the ease

of imagery

earthshine

'90s kid nostalgia cartoon grunge acid wash apathy

'00s baby disney channel terrorism alt soy resentment

self-help section

is there anything

I'm doing right

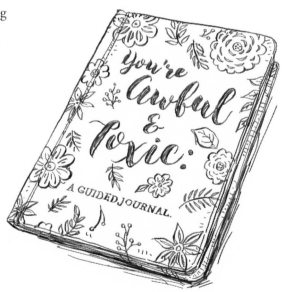

mercury in retrograde...

she brings the car home

with new dents

cold snap

plus the other joys

of dating a gemini

springleavesnoroomfordebate

eggs   wish

scram   what   I'd

bled   I   said

surface water seeing who we are

n't

reCAPTCHA

what if I am

a robot

origami—

folding and unfolding

the instructions

every plot a protagonist cemetery

wrong kind of streaming sockeye

tech detox

was the air

always this crisp

agreeing

to share the aux

autumn equinox

lucid

                dreaming

      just

too

        meta

for

                    me

                                    ████████ :

                          the necessary part

                            of suffering

belt holes

then

and now

tripping hard...

they assure me life is

totally like that bruh

long distance—

settling

for the thought

finding the

openness more and

more oolong

silverfish/lining

new year, new haik(u)

this year

I WILL...

Endnotes

Honkadori: The concept of referencing, reimagining, updating, or corrupting a previously published haiku or senryu to create a new version.

Page 21: A reworking of Ezra Pound's famous quasi-haiku poem "In a Station of the Metro," which appeared in the April 1914 issue of *Poetry*.

Page 41: Even those without an interest in the haiku form have likely seen this poem in print or on the unfashionable t-shirts it later inspired. Its origins have been the source of much conjecture, but renowned haiku poet and scholar Michael Dylan Welch attributes it to Rolf Nelson of Dallas, Texas, circa 2006 (graceguts.com). Here, I've used the "Mocking SpongeBob" meme text format to poke fun at this poem's continued prevalence and its indirect propagation of the outdated 5-7-5 structure.

Page 55: The first poem in my miniature "masters series" sequence is Hokusai's "a poppy blooms." Most know Hokusai for his "Wave" painting, but he wrote poetry as well. The goal with this set is to look at what these masters might have written about had they shared our current (degenerate) sensibilities.

Page 55: Shiki's final haiku, written just before his passing in 1902. Death poems are something of a fascination within the haiku community, with books like Yoel Hoffman's *Japanese Death Poems: Written by Zen Monks and Haiku Poets on the Verge of Death* (Tuttle, 1998) exploring their range and historical significance. I cannot verify whether or not he would've liked eating ass. But I'd like to speculate ;)

Page 55: A "masters series" wouldn't be complete without a reference to the venerable Buson. Sadly, I can't provide the original form of this 1783 poem here, 'cause I'd likely get sued for copyright infringement!

Page 56: A corruption of Bashō's famed "frog pond" poem from 1686. It's something of a rite of passage to try your own take on this one, so my contribution to this tradition was to imagine a version rendered exclusively in emojis. I just hope Bashō isn't spinning in his grave.

Page 90: The "zaddy" poem was written in collaboration with the talented Antoinette Cheung.

Prior Publication Credits

Modern Haiku
Frogpond
The Heron's Nest
Presence
Prune Juice
Haiku Canada Review
Cathexis Northwest Press
The Lyre
Human/Kind
Trash Panda
Kingfisher
Autumn Moon Haiku Journal
Failed Haiku
Under the Bashō
Poetry Pea
2022 Golden Haiku Contest (Commendation)

Note: Some previously published poems have
been altered for this collection.

More Praise for *eggplants & teardrops*

"*eggplants & teardrops* pushes the boundaries of what
we consider English-language haiku and senryu. Using
unconventional and contemporary language, Barry makes the
genre more accessible to a new and younger audience, all the
while establishing a unique voice that is all his own."

Bryan Rickert, Co-editor of *Failed Haiku*

"One doesn't have to look long and hard in this collection
to find literary gems that delight with their sardonic wit.
Aaron has shown that it's truly not the size that matters—these
poems, though small, offer penetrating observations about
the hot mess that is the human experience. For those who need
to know that they are not alone in their insecurities and angst,
this collection hits the spot."

Antoinette Cheung, Winner of the 2021 Betty Drevniok Award

"Infused with a blend of humour and the challenges of our
times, *eggplants & teardrops* offers provocative and surprising
juxtapositions that might have us thinking twice about the
influence of technology on humanity as we know it."

Jacob D. Salzer, Author of *Unplugged— Haiku & Tanka*

"Our post-COVID, post-postmodern society is brimming with more contrasts and contradictions than ever, and Barry's haiku sublimely reveal and explore these conflicts using cleverness, humour, and, when needed, sincerity."

Edward Cody Huddleston, Author of *Wildflowers in a Vase*

"Luminously intense, sympathetically comedic. And the illustrations serve to enhance these qualities every step of the way."

Hemapriya Chellappan, Co-editor of *the QuillS*

"Here is a twenty-something voice that brings to mind Canadian haiku forerunners such as LeRoy Gorman and Dorothy Howard, who experimented with new formats and content. Several decades later, with his Gen-Y eye cast on a very different world, Aaron Barry has delivered a waggish, punchy, and poignant collection of imaginatively conceived poems."

Vicki McCullough, Editor of *Sisyphus: Haiku Work of Anna Vakar*

"Wonderfully subversive and innovative. It's hard to put this collection down."

Nicholas Klacsanzky, founder of *Haiku Commentary*

Aaron Barry is said to look like a poor man's Penn Badgley, and he's perfectly okay with that. His haiku and senryu have appeared in many of English-language haiku's most prestigious magazines and have placed in several international competitions, including the 2019 VCBF Haiku Invitational and The Haiku Foundation's 2021 Touchstone Award for Best Individual Poems. Aaron barely affords rent in Burnaby, BC, Canada.

Find him on IG @aaronmbarry or @zennialhaiku

Made in United States
North Haven, CT
17 November 2022